what is a FRIEND?

WRITTEN BY M.H. CLARK * DESIGNED BY HEIDI RODRIGUEZ

what is a friend?

SHE'S SOMEONE YOU CAN COUNT ON. SHE'S SOMEONE YOU LOOK FORWARD TO. SHE'S SIMPLY WONDERFUL, BUT SHE'S BRILLIANTLY COMPLEX. AND SHE MAKES A DIFFERENCE IN THE WORLD AROUND HER, EVERY SINGLE DAY. SHE'S ALWAYS TRULY, BEAUTIFULLY, UTTERLY HERSELF, AND THAT IS A VERY GOOD THING.

SHE IS JUST EXACTLY
LIKE NOTHING THE WORLD
HAS EVER SEEN BEFORE

SHE'S A DREAMER,
A DOER, A THINKER.
SHE SEES POSSIBILITY
EVERYWHERE.

ring

SHE KEEPS HER SPIRIT OPEN.
SHE LOOKS FORWARD
TO TOMORROW. SHE BELIEVES
IN HER POTENTIAL.

SHE BRINGS GREAT MEANING
TO SIMPLE THINGS BECAUSE SHE
FILLS THEM WITH HERSELF.

gen

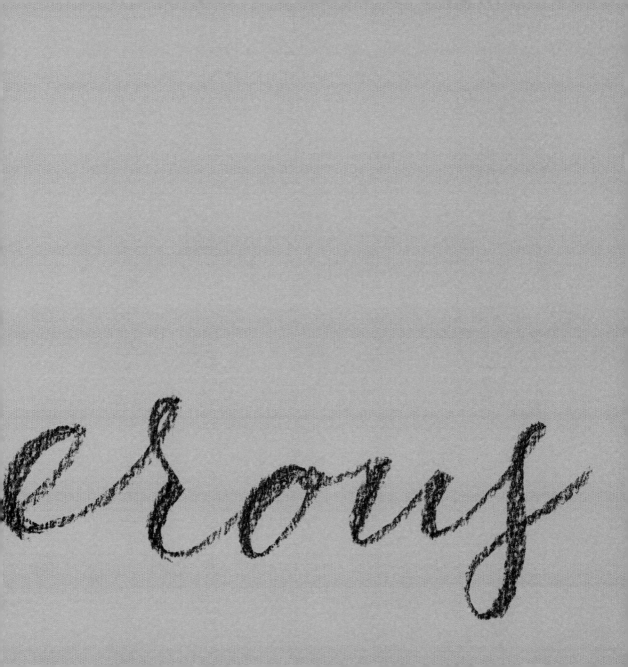

THINGS ARE
ALWAYS BETTER WHEN
SHE'S AROUND.

WHAT IS A FRIEND?

She's someone
you look forward
to seeing.

SHE EMBRACES LIFE. SHE
HAS A HABIT OF SAYING YES
TO BIG CHANCES, BOLD CHOICES,
AND GOOD THINGS.

ONG

SHE LIVES WITH INTENTION.
SHE FIGHTS FOR WHAT
MATTERS. SHE MAKES EACH
DAY HER OWN.

SHE IS THE PERFECT
BLEND OF SILLINESS
AND SERIOUSNESS.

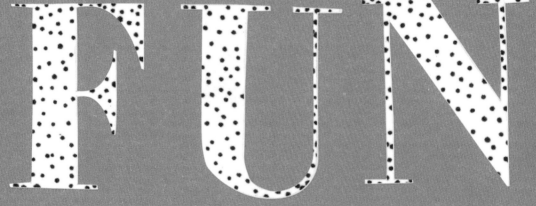

JUST THE POSSIBILITY
OF SEEING HER MEANS
GOOD THINGS ARE ON
THEIR WAY.

SHE MAKES HER OWN TRUTH.
SHE PUSHES THE LIMITS.
SHE REDEFINES WHAT'S POSSIBLE.

WHAT IS A FRIEND?

She's a big part
of everything
that's good in
the world.

SHE GIVES FREELY AND
SHE LISTENS CAREFULLY AND SHE
LOVES WITH ALL HER HEART.

HER ENTHUSIASM
IS CONTAGIOUS.
HER LAUGH CREATES
MORE LAUGHTER.

IN HER COMPANY,
MOMENTS BECOME
MEMORIES.

SHE MAKES TIME
FOR CELEBRATIONS
OF ALL SIZES AND
PEOPLE WHO MATTER.

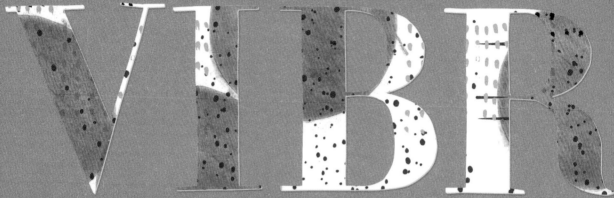

ANT

SHE BRIGHTENS
EVERYTHING AROUND HER
WITH A SPARK
THAT'S ALL HER OWN.

WHAT IS A FRIEND?

She's someone you want to be around.

SHE IS A PERFECT EXAMPLE
OF WHAT IT LOOKS LIKE WHEN
BEAUTY MEETS SUBSTANCE.

SHE BRINGS ALL OF
HERSELF TO THE WORLD.
AND SHE GIVES OTHERS A
CHANCE TO DO THE SAME.

SHE DOES GOOD THINGS
WITH HER TIME, HER
ENERGY, AND HER HEART.

THE CHALLENGES SHE
FACES ONLY SERVE TO
REVEAL HER STRENGTH
AND CAPABILITY.

resilient

SHE KNOWS THAT LIFE
ISN'T PERFECT. SHE LOVES
EVERY LITTLE BIT OF IT
JUST THE SAME.

SHE ADDS LIGHT AND
LIFE TO HER DAYS. SHE
BUILDS HER OWN WORLD
SHE SETTLES FOR MORE

derful

WHAT IS A FRIEND?

She's someone worth celebrating

what is
a friend?

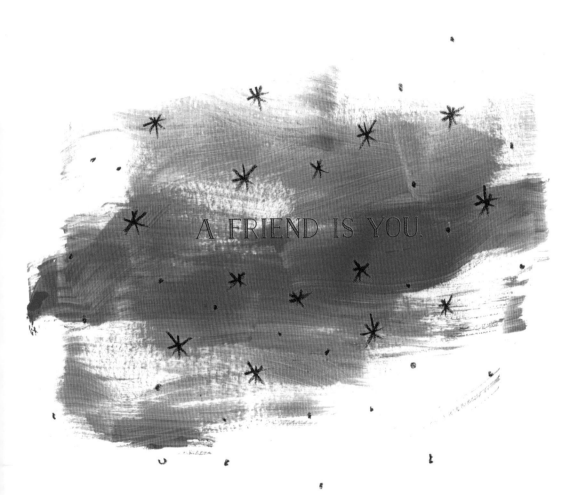

A FRIEND IS YOU.

COMPENDIUM®

live inspired

WITH SPECIAL
THANKS TO THE ENTIRE
COMPENDIUM FAMILY.

CREDITS:

WRITTEN BY: M.H. CLARK

DESIGNED BY: HEIDI RODRIGUEZ

EDITED BY: AMELIA RIEDLER

CREATIVE DIRECTION BY: JULIE FLAHIFF

ISBN: 978-1-938298-56-1

4th printing. Printed in China with soy inks.